Live
Life
Loving.

A Collection of Poems

Jalissa Monique Brown

Contact:

Email: jalissabooks@gmail.com

Twitter: @sexywomenread

 Instagram: @sexywomenread

Facebook: Jalissa Brown

#LiveLifeLoving

For information about special promotions for bulk purchases, please contact the author through email jalissabooks@gmail.com

For information regarding merchandise and apparel associated with the author's books please contact the author through email jalissabooks@gmail.com or visit the author's social media pages listed under contact information.

The author is available for speaking events. For inquires please contact the author through email jalissabooks@gmail.com

ISBN: 978-0-578-17737-3 (printed book)

ISBN: ISBN: 978-0-578-17738-0 (eBook)

Manufactured in the United States of America

Dedication & Special Thanks:

I would like to dedicate this book to my parents, James and Christine Bell. They have always encouraged me to follow my dreams. My parents instilled the values of having faith and working hard to accomplish whatever I set my mind to do. They have truly been my support system during this journey of establishing my writing career.

I would like to also dedicate this book to my sister, Talissa Brown. She is my inspiration and my continued motivation to walk in my purpose and to tell my story.

To all of my family and close friends, thank you for accepting me for me and putting up with this big imagination I have!

I would like to thank every reader and lover for your support. Remember, live life loving!

Dear lovers,

Thank you for taking the time to read about the love I've had, have, and would like to have. I hope you read these poems with an open heart and become inspired to tell your story too. Happy reading!

Love,

Jalissa Monique Brown

Poems by Title:

Poems by Title (continued):

"Whoever has my commands and keeps them is the one who loves me. The one who loves me will be loved by my Father, and I too will love them and show myself to them."

John 14:21 (NIV)

Greatest Love of All

Sins I've committed should not be forgiven,

Yet, your only son died so that I could be a living witness.

A witness of your grace,

A living testimony of your mercy,

God I know you love me,

And I know that you will never hurt me.

Your love is the greatest of all,

Agape,

A love I don't even deserve.

Undeserving when I turned my back

And filled my heart with doubt,

Lord knows my pain and my many sufferings

Because you know my every thought.

Your thoughts of me are good

And never evil

For I was made in your very image,

When they said I couldn't,

You said I could

Because through you

 I can do all things.

Your love is the greatest of all,

Agape,

A love I don't even deserve.

When I disappoint you

 Time after time,

 You remain a forgiving God,

You are my protector,

Shielding me from the very things that come to destroy me.

Holy is The Lamb,

The blessed Lamb of God,

Your love endures

And eases all of my pain,

For I was born into sin,

Yet because I believe in you I was made clean.

Your love is the greatest of all,

Agape,

A love I don't even deserve.

"When you have love, don't let go.

Enjoy the ride. Grip the bars of the

roller coaster of life so tight that

calluses form to remind you of the

ride."

Loving You

Loving you just feels so right,

The thoughts of you make sweet dreams sweeter at night.

Being with you confirms God answers when I pray,

For you are everything I've longed for both night and day.

Warm embraces turned into cold fronts in the form of a change in heart,

They told us time heals and the solution was time apart.

It all sounded scary but we decided it was worth the try,

You looked into my eyes and read my soul, deep down you knew I didn't want to say goodbye.

Months went by and those cold fronts turned frozen,

It was when I saw you with her that I knew I was not the one you

had chosen.

You looked at her like you had once looked at me,

I stood there in my puddle of confusion thinking about our plans

of a future and starting a family.

Butterflies

The butterflies in our bellies turned sick,

There's an issue with their wings,

There's no longer a flutter of happiness

Or kicks of joy.

Wings have been clipped,

 Torn,

And tainted with disappointment

That resonates from our bellies,

Those same bellies

Were once filled

With the flapping of love and hope,

Along with longing and desire.

Once upon a time,

My butterflies and your butterflies

Flew around in unison,

They once moved from side to side,

Filling us with a feeling

That landed in our hearts.

The butterfly wings no longer work,

Therefore our hearts beat at a different pace,

This was all because of the issue with the butterflies

And their wings.

"Let love flourish in the garden of your heart. Let rain shower upon your soul and get drenched in sweet kisses."

When You Told Me

When you told me that you loved me, I did not feel the same,

I will never forget the disappointment and hurt you felt, later the shame.

I disregarded the true essence in what you were really saying to me,

Now all I want is for you to still love me and claim your position back in my destiny.

When you told me what you had felt, I took it all for granted,

Crushing your ego while pushing you into her arms, I now regret it.

I had never planned on hurting you; I promise I was only afraid,

Never meaning for you to take it personal, trust me you're all that

I crave.

Lacking the power to make it all right, I wished upon a star time

and time again,

Confused with every human emotion, not accepting your love for

me could possibly have an end.

If I can't have you in the flesh, I'll settle for when we meet at

night.

Every night, the same time as I close my eyes tight.

Having you in my dreams matter most than not having you at all,

Understanding the feeling now, I have enjoyed the fall.

I've fallen completely in love with you from a distance,

Things are different now because she has your last name, and all I

have is the feeling of missing.

When you told me that you loved me, I had no appreciation for your words harping from your heart,

I long to hear those words again, you loving me in this lifetime will always be the best part.

So many times I've thought about if I could take back the hands of time,

The only thing that comes to mind, is declaring that you were mine.

Under Construction

Personal renaissance,

 A rebirth of self,

I've been trying to avoid my soul's death.

From vibrant colors

To now gray

Almost charcoal black,

I vowed to do anything

To get those colors back.

Second chance at what could have been,

Going forth with what should have been.

Loving myself

Turned out to be much harder than hating myself,

Choosing the latter

Because of a broken heart and torn spirit,

Attempting to remove what felt like a dagger in my chest.

Not quite standing,

But still not completely fallen to the earth,

I am under construction,

Dealing with all the repercussions of not knowing my worth.

I had more lows than I did ups,

Allowing the enemy to tilt my crown,

Little did he know the power of the Father's love

And that titling my crown

Did not equate to knocking it down.

The crown that I was promised

Because I was chosen to be a child of The King,

He saved me from complete self-destruction,

Washed me in his blood,

A spiritual cleansing.

Thank God for forgiving me

For all the things I have done,

Thank God just for me,

He gave his only begotten son.

Now avoiding all roads leading to self-destruction,

I pray this prayer

That I remain under construction.

"Not forgiving is the doormat to

where bitterness resides, and

hatred is its neighbor."

The Promise

I promise to never let you down,

And if I do,

Please forgive me.

I could never intentionally hurt you,

You're everything to me.

You're the star that shines my world;

You're even the fire that burn in the depths of my soul.

I promise to never let you down

And if I do,

Please forgive me,

Because of you I'm a better me.

I could never hurt you intentionally,

 Because that would be like hurting me.

You're the star that shines my world;

You're even the fire that burn in the depths of my soul.

I promise.

Everything

Then you came into my life,

I can see myself being your wife.

You've turned my world upside down,

I'm so addicted, wanting you always to be around.

I have to have you,

No, I need you.

I yearn for your touch,

I can't help I love you so much.

Before you, all I wanted was to feel something,

Now with you, I feel it all, everything.

I Dance For You, You Dance For Me

If you want my loving, then I'll give it freely,

As long as I dance for you, promise you'll dance for me.

Fulfill your dreams, every last fantasy,

Let's go to this place that surpasses ecstasy.

Can we make it last forever and ever?

I can see your effort, every last endeavor.

I am impressed with what I see,

You took me there, I feel like we are one entity.

Can't you hear it, the sound of your heart, my heart?

Our hearts beat in unison in hopes we will never part.

I can hear the sounds of our souls whispering from within,

They are vowing to always be together, for there's no end.

Because of you, because of us, I've entered a trance,

I will forever remember this dance.

I dance for you, just for you solely,

As long as I dance for you, promise you'll dance for me.

Imagine all bad things coming to an end,

Then, would it be possible for us all to ascend?

A world without war,

No children crying, nor hungry, nor poor.

Create with me a world where dance is our token,

A prized token ensuring hearts will forever go unbroken.

Dancing into a life full of happiness, turned bliss,

If you can imagine, then dance to this.

No One

No one would ever understand how much I put my own self

through,

It was to prove to them I could actually be with you.

I'm to blame as well as your insecurity,

Quickly it manifested into my reality.

Fantasy turned bad romance, beyond tragedy,

I lied to myself believing in this catastrophe.

"Loving yourself is the beginning of an endless love affair because it's guaranteed that you'll have yourself forever."

December

December was when I came to the realization he was heartless,

he was mean,

December was when he told me he messed up and that I was his

queen.

December was when I knew I cared for him more than I led him to

believe,

December was when he asked for forgiveness and said he would

do anything to achieve.

December was when I questioned if he really cared for me and

questioned his intent,

December was when I reevaluated all of the energy and time spent.

December was when I decided I wanted more and needed to see more for believing,

December was when it was that time of the year, yes tis the season, but also cuffing season.

December was when I made the decision to leave him in the past,

December was when I knew that decision would never last.

Drowning In Life's Ocean

Drowning in Life's Ocean,

Seasick off of this up and down motion.

Waves of past disappointments

Laced with pieces from my heart,

The only thing that has remained constant

Is me knowing that you are near.

Close enough to feel like the cool breeze

Once it hits my shoulders,

Close enough to smell like the salt

From the waters.

Swimming towards the deep end

Against the currents of lies he once told,

Even against the currents of deceit I still hold.

Almost out of breath,

I hear your voice;

It was in the sound of the ocean,

That's how I knew,

Drowning in life's ocean

In that very moment it had been worth it,

If it meant being with you.

Memory of Us

You wanted me just as much as I wanted you,

Tell me why we both fought it; look at all we have been through.

I played this game of pretending that I didn't need you,

The funny thing is without you, I don't know what I would do.

I attempt to move on; maybe it will come to pass,

Despite what I may try, the memory of us will always be present,

never in the past.

"Break-ups and make-ups are the best teachers of the human behavior."

Carolina Loving

Succulent aromas of soul,

Baked, smothered, and fried,

Added sugar, tea bags and lemons,

Quenching my thirst I have for you.

Sweet nectar dripping,

Preserving of apples and peeling of pears,

Swinging from trees straight into your arms.

Fanning of mosquitoes,

 Sweat beads racing down,

Landing on my lower back,

It becomes a resting area for the very hands I long to hold me.

Scuppernong juice sticking to your skin,

Gathering seeds from watermelons,

Kissing you tastes like the morning dew.

Your hands embrace me,

Holding me tighter,

Like the squeezing of fresh oranges on Sunday mornings.

Summer days were the best days, winter, fall, and spring too,

Sunshine, high tides, and fall colors paint our views.

Collecting of seashells,

Climbing of mountains, and building bonfires,

Every moment with you

Equates to the fireworks at the end of state fairs and festivals.

Baseball and Friday night lights,

Cheering in the stands,

Having you as mine

 Feels like wining queen on homecoming and prom night.

Back roads, dirt paths, and ranch houses all in line,

We chose the pickup truck instead of the Cadillac,

We turn on the radio,

And they play our favorite song.

Prancing of many deer, roaming of bears,

And the soaring of eagles,

When I find myself lost in the woods,

I use the twinkle in your eyes as the North Star.

Carolina Loving and country-style living,

Southern hospitality,

You will forever have an extended stay in my heart.

Feast

They never wanted to see you and me together,

The very thought of us made their blood boil in their self-made pot of jealousy.

A pot that was heated from our passion turned into their flames of envy,

It was never our intention to be the main course of their feast of hatred.

Yet we seasoned the strife they had towards us with bliss and a genuine hope,

A hope that one day, they too could be served a platter of the type of love that only comes from above.

Desert

Abandoned in the desert of heartbreak,

Fortunate enough to have shades to block sunlight,

but nothing to protect my heart.

Looking into the distance,

 I saw no end to this journey without you,

Pure misery,

Only left with the water that ran through my body,

Dehydrated off constant thoughts of you.

Sweat beads ran down every inch of me,

I wished those had been the tip of your fingers,

The more I walked through the dirt and sand,

I left a trail of footprints that were losing form from my tears.

The rose that appeared in front of me

Reminded me of the beautiful memories we had together,

I plucked the rose to find out that it was really a cactus.

Blood rolled down my index finger,

The same finger used to dial your number so many times before,

I had wished things could have been different;

We had once been in paradise together.

A paradise of love

Filled with exotic fruits and flowers,

Now I was stuck in the middle of the desert alone,

Without you in sight.

Just when exhaustion set in,

More emotionally

Than physically,

An oasis of love appeared immediately.

An abundance of water,

With a taste much sweeter than I had remembered from you,

It was fertile

And full of the emotions I no longer could possess myself.

I jumped in wholeheartedly

Without anything else to lose,

In the middle of my drought, and journey through the desert,

The love of God became my haven.

Platform

I watched you from the platform, waiting for the Brooklyn bound

A,

I'll never forget anything about that day.

You paced back and forth, stepping on the yellow line,

You peeped to see if the train was coming; in confusion you

reread the sign.

Ensuring you were on the right side, in hopes of reaching your

destination,

Still watching you, I hid behind the young couple as they stole

sweet kisses; your presence alone gave me an unreal sensation.

You seemed to be in a hurry, looking constantly at your wrist, I

wanted you to notice me so desperately,

The shirt that wrapped around your body swayed with the wind

from the incoming train, wishing you would just look at me.

The train doors opened, you entered, and I remained stuck in the

quicksand of your aura,

I missed my train that day; I prayed I would see you tomorrow.

Midnight Riding

I woke up in the western part of my city this morning,

The smell of midnight kisses still roam through the air.

I peep from the covers simultaneously pinching myself,

I was in disbelief of the events that occurred last night.

Straight from a movie, you took me riding,

I held on tight and glued my body to yours.

Adrenaline and my desire for you was rising,

Those were the results of midnight riding.

"Love is like a painting, all the colors mix together to make a beautiful masterpiece, God is the artist. God is love."

Canvas

Use me as your canvas,

Paint me exactly how you would like.

Color me as you see me,

Create your innermost feelings.

Yellow, red, a little blue,

I trust your artistry.

Strokes and blotches, don't miss a spot,

Make me into your masterpiece.

Use me as your canvas,

Paint me exactly how you would like.

Before Hello

I was drawn to your smile;

It was an immediate attraction,

I watched how they watched you

And I studied your reaction.

Your presence was potent,

Instead of it drawing me closer,

it made me stand in the distance.

I stood there wondering if you had noticed me and if I had the

slightest chance.

So I stood there

From a far

Watching you,

And then wanting you,

Now needing you,

Mesmerized by every aspect of you,

And by every intricate detail of you.

Your eyes met mine

And I could feel my heart beating the same pace as the vibrations

bouncing from your hello,

Words struggled leaving my mouth,

You asked me to dance,

Fast then slow.

You noticed my nervousness

So you smiled to comfort me,

From that point on

As the music stopped,

No one else in the room was visible

You were all I could see.

Your words enticed me as the night went on,

You spoke to my intellect,

Little did you know what I was thinking,

What you did to me,

Your affect.

You captured more than my attention,

You took my heart as prisoner,

I did not mind

As long as you continued seeking my truth,

Exploring what mattered,

The inner.

Then you did the unthinkable

By unlocking the very door

 I vowed never to open,

You gave me hope

That real still exists,

You made it clear

You could handle what I dared not to share,

The unspoken.

You held the key,

The power to unleash the beast I always kept hidden,

My fears,

The more you spoke proved that you saw me for me

 And not for what I had been in past years.

As the night ended

And flirting continued,

I realized you had me in awe before hello,

I knew you would change my life

The moment you walked through the door.

The Turning of Leaves

The time came and the color of the leaves were turning,

Some yellow, some red but I had only taken notice to this feeling,

this burning.

It was a burning of complete and utter desire,

A desire that derived from a place so deep inside of me, the

flames surpassed fire.

I never knew my soul could vibrate at such a rapid pace,

It started that one fall day, your lips against mine, I remember the

taste.

You left me feeling alive, wanting more, wondering what could be,

Now that we don't speak, I realize the turning of the leaves were

you, then me.

We Never End

You're not here but I can feel your embrace,

If I hold up my hands I swear I can feel your face.

I close my eyes and I can feel your body heat,

Everything inside me starts to rush, and then stop, my heart skips

a beat.

You're not here but I feel you so close,

I want you so much I love you the most.

You're more than my lover, you're my friend,

I long for your kiss and pray to God we never end.

Empty

A basin full of tears I've cried,

There were many days it overflowed because you lied.

You said you would never leave me,

I believed those words whole heartedly.

Thank God for a new day and the sun shining,

Without it, I would have ended up floating in my tears, then

drowning.

Evaporated, now empty, sun dried,

There once was a basin full of the tears I cried.

"Giving someone the sole power of being irreplaceable in your life is like giving them a dictatorship role to your soul."

Scab

Falling off the ride of love,

Scraping every inch of my heart and soul.

Puss of hurt oozes from the very depths of what was once a

bubble of bliss,

Blood runs down staining the sheets where you use to hold me.

Now I'm searching for a bandage, but none seems to fit,

Nothing can hold the overflow of emotions.

It settles as an open wound, soon to be scab,

Healing will come, but the more I'm without you there's a picking

of that scab.

It's conveniently situated where you once kissed,

Keeping the scab means keeping part of you.

Time

Time may heal, but too much time can kill,

It could kill the very seed within our garden of love.

That one seed holds the power, the potential for us to last

forever,

I don't want to have time a part.

I'm afraid time would poison the flowers of our souls,

Time may heal, but too much time can kill.

Wildflower

You found me where the wildflowers grow,

In a random place of longing and amongst the weeds and dirt.

You bent down to get a closer look,

Then you stared into the stem of my soul.

You admired my beauty despite the conditions of my petals,

Some were torn, others were weathered.

You found me where the wildflowers grow,

Roadside,

Overlooked,

Not like the other flowers found in storefronts.

Many had passed me by,

I often wondered if I was worthy to be plucked and carried home,

Unbeknownst to me,

I had been positioned in your life's path

To be distinguished from the rest.

I was far from the meadows

And completely opposite of any rose bush,

Yet, I was the one you chose, wild and free.

Love Will Last

Years may surely past,

But our love will last.

There's no need to say our goodbyes

Because our souls will forever have ties,

We separated,

Not for a lacking there of,

It was more so because we realized it was more than love.

Our likes became love,

Then lust

Now obsession,

Words were said in a jealous rage

Then the confession.

I hurt you

Because you hurt me,

Never in a million years did I think this would be,

Years may surely past,

But our love will last.

Love Song

Keys of happiness streaming from what feels good and what feels
nice,

All based upon this song, this melody we call life.

See, it's not just any song, it's our song, it's the type of song that
will make you cry,

Have you asking what you did to deserve this sound of love,

asking God why?

It's not every day one can whistle what's really in their hearts,

Some people live a lifetime never getting to that part.

This song is compiled of up tempos and highs,

It'll leave you thanking everything that resides in the skies.

On that note, this song, our song is also hosted with a chorus of
soulful tones and lows,

Filled with tempos and arrangements only God knows.

Showered in crescendos of passion it's the only song I'll sing,

Sounds of love that fills hearts everlasting.

Musical notes of promises and sharps of compromises,

A love song so deep, it'll have you making ultimate sacrifices.

Our song, this love song, it's about you and I

A blessed harmony where whole notes of desire never die.

There's a humming in our spirits, falsetto in our souls, and the same drum beats in our hearts,

We repeat that same rhythm because that's our favorite part.

Affection, my kisses, and your touch are the keys, octave after octave, allowing God to be our conductor,

Awaiting the day they ask about our song, this love song, Encore!

"Despite the all the heartbreaks,

the worst of all is never finding

love."

About the Author

Jalissa Monique Brown is a writer born and raised in North Carolina. She is a graduate of the University of North Carolina at Greensboro, with a Bachelor of Arts degree in International and Global Studies. She also minored in Political Science, while strengthening her language skills in Spanish and French. Her studies concentrated on culture and human rights.

Her small town roots inspired her to travel and see the world she always read about as a child. One of her first jobs was a library page at the Public Library in her hometown.

After graduating college she moved to New York City, where she now resides. She spends her time traveling, reading many books and writing about her experiences. This is her first published book. Her second book is entitled: *Her Bare Soul: Poems From An African American Woman's Perspective.*

Her message to the world is "live life loving".

www.ingramcontent.com/pod-product-compliance
Lightning Source LLC
Chambersburg PA
CBHW071429040426
42445CB00012BA/1307